ROADS FOR PROSPERITY

Presented to Parliament by the Secretary of State for Transport by Command of Her Majesty May 1989

LONDON
HER MAJESTY'S STATIONERY OFFICE

Cm 693   £5.20 net

Cover Photograph
M1 / M62
Lofthouse Interchange
Yorkshire

1. This White Paper announces a greatly expanded motorway and trunk road programme to relieve congestion on the major roads between cities and towns in England. It does not deal with roads within the M25, other conurbations or cities. Schemes worth over £6 billion are to be added, more than doubling the size of the programme.

2. The new programme gives even higher priority to meeting the needs of industry and of other road users for a modern strategic road network which also helps to reduce accidents and to improve the environment. It shows the Government's commitment to the provision of transport infrastructure suited to the single market and the other competitive challenges of the 1990s and beyond.

3. The expanded programme announced in this White Paper will improve the inter-urban motorway and trunk road network by reducing journey times and increasing the reliability of road travel. It is a vital further boost for British industry. The measures proposed will provide the means to improve the country's economic geography, increasing opportunities for the less favoured areas, assisting urban regeneration and helping the more prosperous areas to cope with growth. The programme will be reviewed and supplemented as circumstances and the needs of road users develop.

ROAD CONGESTION

4. There has been unprecedented sustained economic growth in recent years. One of the consequences has been very large increases in the demand for all forms of transport - air, rail and road. These increases have been very much higher than anyone forecast or expected.

5. Traffic on the roads has increased by 35 per cent since 1980, with particularly high growth on motorways (where traffic has nearly doubled) and on trunk roads (where traffic has increased by a half). In the same period the number of vehicles on the roads has increased by three million, to over twenty-three million.

6. Road congestion is bad for the economy. It imposes high costs on industry and other road users, by wasting time, delaying deliveries and reducing reliability. Various estimates have been made of these economic costs of road congestion. There is no way of making accurate overall estimates, but it is clear that the costs are very high.

7. Road congestion is also bad for the environment and bad for safety. It encourages traffic to use unsuitable roads, damaging the quality of life of people who live nearby, wasting fuel and increasing the number of accidents.

8. People realise that there will be delays when there are accidents, when there are roadworks, or at some peak travel times, like rush hours in the big cities and Bank Holiday Mondays. Much can be done in urban areas by using modern techniques of traffic management to ease congestion and delays; but people accept that the scope is limited.

9. Road users do not expect, however, to endure stop-start conditions on ordinary journeys between cities. This is happening now. Unless action is taken, it will get worse as high economic growth continues, reflecting the long-term structural improvements in the economy achieved under this Government.

OPTIONS FOR RELIEVING CONGESTION

10. The Government has considered various ways to eliminate unacceptable levels of congestion on inter-urban roads.

11. The railways help by providing services which passengers and freight customers wish to use. British Rail, assisted by record levels of investment, are attracting more and more passengers. The prospects for rail freight are better than for many years with the opportunity offered by the Channel Tunnel and in certain cases grants are available under Section 8 of the Railways Act 1974 for rail freight handling facilities to help keep lorries off unsuitable roads. Yet even with the continued expansion of rail, it cannot take other than a small part of the increase in demand for transport overall.

12. Road and rail by and large serve different markets, and for most traffic the one cannot readily be substituted for the other. Short freight movements are usually best suited to road; over 65% of loaded road freight journeys are of 50 miles or less.

13. The different scale of road and rail activity is also important. Road transport is responsible for twelve times more passenger travel and ten times more freight movement than rail. A 50 per cent increase in rail traffic would reduce road traffic by less than 5 per cent. Rail has an important contribution to make but it is not the panacea for congestion on inter-urban roads.

14. Traffic management can help to make maximum safe use of the network. Its greatest contribution is and will continue to be in city and town centres. It can also help in the maximum safe use of motorways and trunk roads, for example through variable message systems or by signalled access control; but this contribution cannot hope to make much impact on the very large increases in traffic now forecast.

15. Another option would be to impose higher taxes on road users generally to reduce demand. But road users already pay some three times the annual cost of road construction and maintenance in taxes directly related to the ownership and use of vehicles.

16. The Government's conclusion is that the main way in which to deal with growing and forecast inter-urban road congestion is by widening existing roads and building new roads in a greatly expanded road programme. The scale of the problem is such that it can be relieved only by a step-change in both the size and the composition of the programme.

PRESENT PLANS

17. Already the Government has acted. Since 1979, 264 trunk road schemes have been completed, adding 900 miles to the network. Investment is nearly 60 per cent higher in real terms than in 1979. At the moment, there are some 330 schemes in the trunk road programme, with a works value of over £5 billion.

18. Provision for trunk roads was expanded in the most recent Public Expenditure White Paper (Cm 608). For the next three years, total Roads Vote provision is 22 per cent higher in real terms than over the last three years. In this financial year (1989/90) provision for new construction is 20 per cent higher than last year.

19. This is a large programme, bestowing great benefits including very high economic returns and some relief from congestion. Quantifiable economic benefits from road schemes are on average nearly twice the cost of construction. Nevertheless, the scale and cost of present and prospective road congestion is so great that the Government has fundamentally re-examined the road programme.

NEW TRAFFIC FORECASTS

20. The Government is announcing today new national road traffic forecasts. The Annex summarises these. Total traffic is forecast to increase by between 83 per cent and 142 per cent by the year 2025, compared with 1988.

21. These forecasts are considerably higher than the previous forecasts issued in 1984. The new traffic forecasts are higher largely as the result of higher forecast economic growth. Economic growth means that we produce and consume more and better goods and services. These increase demand for transport. No major technical change is expected to upset the dominance of road transport in the timescale considered.

22. Both the number of cars and their use will grow. As people become more prosperous they choose to acquire cars and to use them. There are still significantly fewer cars per head in this country than in the United States, France and the Federal Republic of Germany. Social factors are also at work, especially the increasing number of women and older people driving cars.

23. Road planning and investment are long-term. Forecasting over the long periods covered in the national traffic forecasts is therefore necessary. There is uncertainty associated with forecasts for so long a period ahead. Therefore a wide range of outcomes has to be considered. The ranges in the new forecasts reflect the results of using "high" and "low" economic growth rates of broadly 3 per cent and 2 per cent per annum respectively.

THE EFFECT OF HIGHER TRAFFIC GROWTH ON CONGESTION

24. The higher traffic now forecast would make traffic congestion on the main inter-urban routes significantly worse. A systematic review of the trunk road network has therefore been undertaken. This review considered the need for measures on motorways wherever in weekday peak hours traffic is regularly forced into stop-start operation and minor incidents cause considerable delay. Such conditions, and their equivalent on other trunk roads, are already widely experienced and, without relief measures, will become much more widespread. The review has considered the need for improvement, taking account of value for money, wherever these conditions occur or are forecast to occur on inter-urban roads.

25. The prospect - unless further action is taken - is one of growing congestion progressively spreading through the key routes in the national network, including those which are most important to industry. There would also be local congestion in other parts of the network. The consequence would be ever increasing delays and costs, making British industry less able to compete internationally, as well as great inconvenience and cost for other road users. The Government is not willing to accept this outcome.

OBJECTIVES OF THE EXPANDED ROAD PROGRAMME

26. The fundamental objectives of the trunk road programme are unchanged. These are:

- to assist economic growth by reducing transport costs

- to improve the environment by removing through traffic from unsuitable roads in towns and villages

- to enhance road safety.

27. The new emphasis on relieving inter-urban congestion announced in this White Paper is consistent with meeting the above objectives. The Government remains committed to ensuring that it gets good value for money in undertaking schemes. With predicted traffic growth the already considerable costs of congestion will grow. While it is not possible or economic to remove all congestion, the case for investment on a substantial scale to relieve congestion on the major inter-urban routes is clear.

THE EXPANDED PROGRAMME

Size of the Programme

28. Through assessment of the problems and opportunities on a route-by-route basis, an expanded programme of over £6 billion has been identified. When this is added to the existing programme the total road programme will be over £12 billion.

29. Thus the trunk road programme will be more than doubled. The Government is committed to construction of a programme of this size and will be increasing annual expenditure on the road programme. The amount and timing of additional expenditure will be for decision in the Public Expenditure Survey in the usual way. Adequate provision will also continue to be made for cost-effective road maintenance.

30. The new programme will add over 2,700 miles of new or widened roads to the trunk road network.

Schemes in the Programme

31. The schemes added to the programme are listed in Table 1 and their location, together with existing schemes, is shown on the map appended to this White Paper. In addition, there are a number of corridors where there is a prima facie case for further investigation, with a view to provision of further capacity in the longer term, possibly including new strategic routes. These corridors for further investigation are listed in Table 2.

32. A full Roads Report later in the year will set out the complete road programme in detail with supporting information.

Balance of the Programme

33. The schemes now added, and the schemes already in the programme, provide a balanced approach to future road provision. The programme takes account of problems and opportunities on a country-wide basis. All the schemes will provide a mix of economic, environmental and safety benefits.

34. The expanded programme contains important bypass schemes and other projects to deal with local problems of congestion, even where these are away from the biggest industrial centres.

35. But the balance and emphasis of the programme has been switched towards schemes which relieve congestion on the most heavily used parts of the network, particularly those which meet the needs of industry for better communications. This means that the new programme concentrates on relieving congestion on the broad routes followed by the present motorways which have by far the heaviest flows of traffic, especially lorries.

36. The motorway programme already includes completion of the M3, M20, M40 and orbital routes around Birmingham and Manchester as well as over 85 miles of widening schemes. Major improvements to the motorway network added in this White Paper include widening and junction improvements on the M1 between the M25 and the M18 in South Yorkshire, the M4 between the M25 and Reading, the M4/M5 north and west of Bristol, the M6 between the M1 and Manchester, all of the three-lane sections of the M25, the M62 between Manchester and Huddersfield, and parts of the M3, M11, M20, M23, M40, M42, M56 and M63. New motorways are proposed to the west and north of Manchester between the M6 and the M66 and between Chelmsford and the M25.

37. For the A1, it is proposed to extend the southern section of A1(M) from Letchworth to the junction with the M1 - A1 Link in Cambridgeshire, to convert the Redhouse to Hook Moor section in Yorkshire to motorway, to widen the existing A1(M) between M25 and Letchworth and to widen and improve the route from the M1 - A1 Link junction to Stamford. Studies will consider the needs of the section of the route between Stamford and the A1(M) south of Doncaster and the longer term requirements of the section between Hook Moor and the A1(M) south of Darlington, where improvements are currently in preparation, and of the northern section of A1(M). This programme will provide the basis for a comprehensive review of the route including investigation of the possibility of full motorway status from London to Tyneside.

38. Major improvements are also proposed for important all-purpose trunk roads. Together with the existing programme, this will lead to the dualling of the A11 between the M11 and Norwich, upgrading of the A12 from Chelmsford to Ipswich, and dualling the remaining length to Lowestoft, dualling of the A47 between Peterborough and Norwich, upgrading the A27 and A259 between Portsmouth and the Channel Tunnel, the A31/A35, A30, A38, and A303 in the south west and the A36/A46 between Southampton and Bath, trunking and improvement of the A350 between the A31 and Poole, and improvements to the A59 in Lancashire and the A628 between Manchester and Sheffield.

39. The east-west corridor north of London between the M40 and the ports of Felixstowe and Harwich is to be developed as a trunk road, building on preparations for the Thame-Stevenage route and the improvement of the A120. Schemes developed by local authorities will be incorporated where appropriate. The route will provide additional links to Stansted Airport and some relief to the M25 by adding essential trunk road capacity in this area of high traffic growth.

40. Studies are proposed for the east-west corridor south of London, for a further Thames crossing east of Dartford, for a route between M3 and M40 to help relieve the south west quadrant of the M25, and across the southern Pennines.

41. Where possible, the initial aim is to increase directly the capacity of existing routes by widening and by improvements to junctions. These improvements will need to be supplemented in some cases by new routes after an interval. On-line widening of motorways will normally be to a maximum of no more than four lanes on each carriageway with associated junction improvements.

The M25 Motorway

42. The M25 is the most heavily used road in the country. It is serving much more traffic than was forecast when the road was planned, and is suffering serious congestion at peak hours. The Government commissioned consulting engineers Rendel, Palmer and Tritton in April 1988 to consider the options. The expanded programme announced in this White Paper includes a proposal for the M25 to be widened to dual 4-lane standards. The consultants' report will be published shortly and the Government will announce further plans for action later in the year.

Economic Effects

43. The schemes in the expanded programme are projected to achieve a high economic return, at least comparable with the return expected from the schemes in the present programme especially in view of fast-increasing traffic. These schemes will help to keep industrial and commercial costs down, and help British firms to compete. They will help to offset the disadvantage which British industry suffers from being on the geographical periphery of the European Community. They will help British firms to make deliveries reliably, and "just in time".

Environment

44. New roads take traffic away from places where it should not be, helping to protect local communities and buildings and making life tolerable in residential areas and shopping streets. For these reasons, many communities are anxious to have bypasses. Where new roads are built particular care is taken to fit the road and structures into the landscape and to take all reasonable measures to minimise any adverse effects. The emphasis in the expanded programme on increasing the capacity of existing routes will help to minimise its impact on the environment. Protecting and enhancing the environment will continue to be a major feature of the Government's road building plans, complementing the commitment to eliminate lead from petrol and secure radical reductions in gaseous emissions and noise.

Safety

45. New roads are safer roads. An expanded trunk road programme will mean quicker reductions in casualties and contribute to the Government's objective of reducing casualties by one third by 2000. At the same time the programme of small local safety schemes will be stepped up.

Timing and Delivery of the Expanded Programme

46. Preparation of the expanded programme will be started immediately. Consulting engineers will be appointed as soon as possible to work up, prepare and design individual schemes.

47. Motorway widening schemes will dominate the early stages of the expanded programme. It is in general faster and easier to widen existing roads than to build entirely new roads, so the emphasis on widening will help to speed up construction. Some disruption to road users will be unavoidable but the Government will schedule its work programmes to keep this to a minimum. Where possible, a new approach will be used in which a new carriageway will be built alongside the existing motorway before that is modified to provide the other carriageway.

48. The size and urgency of the new programme means that present ways of administering trunk road construction will no longer be effective for all schemes. As now, the great bulk of detailed preparation and design will be done by consulting engineers. Possible new arrangements to achieve the most effective organisation of consultants and civil servants are being considered. Improvements will come from concentration on the task in hand and from greater efficiency in combining the skills and experience of both the public and private sectors.

49. Administrative procedures are already being speeded up. Targets have been set for reducing by 4 years the average time taken to progress schemes from programme entry to opening for traffic. The rights of individuals and others affected by specific schemes will continue to be protected.

50. The construction industry has responded in the past to the challenges of road building. The Government recognises that the expansion of the road programme will require major adaptations by the industry but is confident that this will be achieved, with publication of a strategic long-term construction programme. Careful consideration will be given to planning so that the workload can be spread to avoid local overheating and difficulties with the supply of materials.

Private Finance

51. The Government will publish shortly a consultation document on private finance for roads which proposes new procedures for private sector roads. The Government wishes to harness the skills and efficiency of the private sector to the maximum extent in the provision of roads. The Government will be ready to consider proposals for the private finance of the schemes listed in this White Paper where this would offer improved value for money and would welcome proposals for other private sector road schemes.

CONCLUSION

52. Effective transport is a vital element of economic growth and prosperity. The continuing advance of our economy and society requires progressive development of the motorway and trunk road network. Now is the time for a large step forward. A major expansion of the Government's programme for building and improving inter-urban roads is being put in hand to meet the forecast needs of traffic into the next century. The Government is committed to taking the programme forward as a matter of urgency.

TABLE 1: ADDITIONS TO THE TRUNK ROAD CONSTRUCTION PROGRAMME

This Table lists sections of route for which additional new construction or improvement is proposed. For many of the sections more than one scheme is involved. (1)

	Proposed Standard (2)	Estimated Works Cost (£ million) (3)	Approximate Length (Miles)
MOTORWAYS			
Existing Routes			
M1 London - Leeds			
Widening between Junctions 6A-32 (M25-M18)	D4	960	145
M621 to M1 Link Road Improvement	D2	7	--
M3 London - Southampton			
Widening between Junctions 2-4	D4	41	12
M4 London - Severn Bridge			
Widening between Junctions 8/9-12	D4	72	17
Widening between Junctions 18-20	D4	85	10
Junction 4A Improvement (Heathrow Spur)	--	6	--
M5 Birmingham - Exeter			
Widening between Junctions 15-21	D4	150	21
Junction 1 Improvement	--	6	--
Junction 2 Improvement	--	6	--
Junction 12 Improvement	--	1	1
Junction 18 Improvement and Avonmouth Relief Road	D2	20	2
M6 Leicestershire - Scottish Border			
Widening between M1 and Junction 4 (M42)	D4	200	24
Widening between Junctions 11-20	D4	480	56
Junction 9 Improvement	--	6	--
Junction 10 Improvement	--	6	--
M11 London - Cambridge			
Widening between Junctions 8-14	D3	81	25
M20 London - Folkestone			
Widening between Junctions 3-5	D4	25	6
M23 London - Crawley			
Widening between Junctions 8-9	D4	30	7
M25 London Orbital			
Widening of dual 3 lane sections	D4	1000	107
M40 London - Birmingham			
Widening between Junctions 1A-4	D4	67	12
M42 Birmingham			
Widening between M5 and M6	D4	185	21
M45 Warwickshire			
A45 Junction Improvement	--	1	--
M56 Manchester - Chester			
Widening between Junctions 4-6	D4	23	2

	Proposed Standard (2)	Estimated Works Cost (£ million) (3)	Approximate Length (Miles)
M62 Merseyside - Humberside			
Widening between Junctions 6-7	D4	14	3
Widening between Junctions 18-24	D4	125	17
M62 (East) to M606 Link Road	S	5	1
Junction 20 Improvement (A627(M))	--	5	--
M63 Manchester Outer Ring Road			
Widening between Junctions 7-9	D4	20	3
M606 Bradford			
A6177 Junction Improvement	--	2	--

New Routes

M25 to Chelmsford	D2	45	11
Greater Manchester Western and Northern Relief Road (M6 to M66) (incorporating M56 Junction 7 to M6 Junction 19 and M62 widening between Junctions 12-18)	D3	300	20
Second Severn Crossing Approach Roads (including links to M4 and M5 and widening of M4 to Almondsbury)	D2/D3	69	10
M1/M62 Lofthouse Interchange Diversion	D2	10	3

A1 LONDON - SCOTTISH BORDER

A1(M)			
Widening between Junctions 1-8	D4/D3	84	30
Widening between Junctions 9-10	D3	10	3
Junction 10 to M1-A1 Link (conversion to motorway)	D3	140	25
Redhouse (Doncaster A1(M)) to Hook Moor (A642 East of Leeds) - (conversion to motorway)	D3	100	17
A1 (all purpose)			
M1-A1 Link to Stamford Widening	D3	60	22
A69 Gateshead Western Bypass Improvement (A1 on completion)	D3	13	7
Junction Improvements at Biggleswade, Black Cat, Blyth, Langford Turn, Markham Moor, Sandy and South of Brampton Roundabout	--	27	4

OTHER TRUNK ROADS

Existing Routes

A2/A282 Dartford - Thurrock Crossing Approach Roads			
Dartford Improvements	D4/D2	27	6
A3 London - Portsmouth			
M25 to B2234 Improvement	D3	22	5
Stoke Road to Hogs Back (Guildford) Improvement	D3	28	3
A5 London - Shrewsbury and Welsh Border			
M1 to South Dunstable Dualling	D2	13	4
North Dunstable to Little Brickhill Dualling	D2	17	11
Towcester Bypass	S	3	2
Weeford to Fazely Improvement	D2	15	3
Corridor Improvements	S	3	4

	Proposed Standard (2)	Estimated Works Cost (£ million) (3)	Approximate Length (Miles)
A6 Luton - Manchester			
Disley and High Lane Bypass	D2	40	5
Great Glen to Desborough Improvement	D2/S	6	4
Kibworth Bypass	S	4	3
Loughborough Bypass	S	21	6
A10 London - King's Lynn			
Cambridge to Ely Widening	D2	20	13
M25 to Hoddesdon Improvement	D2	13	8
Corridor Improvements	S	1	1
A11 Cambridge - Norwich			
Five Ways to Bridgham Heath Dualling	D2	21	15
Attleborough Bypass Dualling	D2	5	3
A12 London - Great Yarmouth			
Chelmsford Bypass widening	D3	24	13
Hatfield Peverel to Witham Widening	D3	4	3
Saxmundham to Lowestoft Widening	D2	22	35
Wickham Market to Farnham Widening	D2	8	5
Corridor Improvements	D2	3	2
A16 Stamford - Grimsby			
Corridor Improvements (Bypasses of East Keal, Fotherby, Ludborough, Stickford)	S	4	4
A17 Newark - King's Lynn			
King's Lynn to Sutton Bridge Widening	D2	12	7
Leadenham to Sleaford Improvement	D2/S	7	6
Sutterton to New Washway Improvement	D2	18	15
A19 Selby - Newcastle			
Norton to Parkway Improvement	D3	12	5
Shipton by Beningbrough Bypass	S	2	1
Thormanby Bypass, North Yorks	S	2	1
A21 London - Hastings			
Flimwell Improvement	D2/S	2	1
Hurst Green Bypass	D2	7	3
Lamberhurst Bypass to Chingley Wood Improvement	D2	6	2
A26 Lewes - Newhaven			
Beddingham to Itford Farm Diversion	S	4	2
A27 Eastbourne - Portsmouth			
Lewes to Polegate Improvement	D2	25	9
Worthing to Lancing Improvement	D3/D2	33	6
A30 Honiton - Penzance			
Honiton to Exeter Improvement	D2	33	12
St. Erth to Newtown Improvement	D2	7	4
Temple to Higher Carblake Improvement	D2	3	3
Zelah to Chiverton Improvement	S	5	4

	Proposed Standard (2)	Estimated Works Cost (£ million) (3)	Approximate Length (Miles)
A31 Southampton - Dorchester			
M27 to Ringwood Improvements	D3	41	13
A35 Dorchester - Honiton			
Wilmington Bypass	S	3	2
Winterbourne Abbas Bypass	S	4	3
Corridor Improvements	D2	1	1
A36/A46 Southampton - Bath			
Codford to Wylye Improvement	D2	2	2
East of Bath to Beckington	D2	46	11
Upper Swainswick to Pennsylvania*	D2	12	3
A38 Birmingham - M1			
A5148 Junction Improvement	--	5	--
Corridor Improvements	S	1	--
A38 Exeter - Bodmin			
Saltash to Trerulefoot Improvement	D2	25	8
A39 Barnstaple - West of Bodmin			
Camelford Bypass	S	4	2
Corridor Improvements	S	5	5
A40 London - Ross-on-Wye			
M50 Gorsley to Longford Improvement*	D2/S	28	12
Corridor Improvements	--	1	--
A41 London - Liverpool			
Corridor Improvements between Chester and M54	S	10	7
A45 Felixstowe - A1 (Cambridgeshire)			
M11 to A10 Widening	D3/D2	10	3
A1 to West of Cambridge Improvement	D2	36	15
Corridor Improvements	D2	4	4
A45 Birmingham - Northampton			
Weedon, Flore and Upper Heyford Bypass*	S	8	4
Junction Improvements, Coventry	--	25	2
A46 Leicester - Lincoln			
Newark (A1133) to Lincoln Improvement	D2	12	8
Newark to Widmerpool Improvement	D2/S	20	17
A47 Leicester - Great Yarmouth			
Peterborough to Norwich Dualling	D2	97	54
A1 to Leics/Northants Boundary (A43) Widening	D2	6	6
Acle Straight Improvement	D2	7	7
East Norton Bypass	S	2	1
A49 Warrington - Ross-on-Wye			
Corridor Improvements	S	38	19
A51 / A52/A500 Chester - M6			
Shavington to Basford Improvement	S	6	4
Corridor Improvements	D2/S	18	8

	Proposed Standard (2)	Estimated Works Cost (£ million) (3)	Approximate Length (Miles)
A52 Derby - Grantham			
Radcliffe-on-Trent to Grantham Improvement	D2/S	20	16
A54/A556 Chester - M6			
M6 to A559 Improvement	D2	9	3
Corridor Improvements	D2/S	7	6
A56 M65-M66			
A682 Junction Improvement	--	5	--
A57/A628 Manchester - Sheffield			
Corridor Improvements between M67 and A616	D2/S	33	16
A59 Merseyside - North Yorkshire			
Ormskirk-Walmer Bridge Improvement	D2	30	11
Preston Southern and Western Bypass	D3/D2	80	10
Corridor Improvements Preston-Skipton	S	6	4
A63 Leeds - Hull			
Castle Street, Hull	D3	8	--
West of A1 Junction, Leeds	D2	30	4
A64 York - Scarborough			
York Bypass to Malton Bypass Dualling	D2	16	12
A65 Leeds - Kendal			
Ilkley Bypass	S	13	3
Corridor Improvements	S	6	3
A127 London - Southend			
M25 to Rayleigh Relief Road (parallel route)	D2	40	19
A140 Ipswich - Norwich			
Scole to Norwich Widening	D2	35	21
A167 Stockton - Chester-Le-Street			
Cock o' the North to Aycliffe Improvement	D2	13	10
A249 Sittingbourne - Sheerness			
Iwade Bypass to Queenborough	D2	37	2
Corridor Improvements	S	2	--
A259 Folkestone - Eastbourne			
Pevensey to Bexhill Improvement	D2	5	2
Corridor Improvements	S	8	5
A303 Andover - Honiton			
Berwick Down to Amesbury Improvement	D2	6	5
Bullington Cross to Andover Improvement	--	3	--
Mere to Wylye Improvement	D2	9	11
A339 Basingstoke - Newbury			
Basingstoke to Newbury Improvements	D3/D2	57	17

	Proposed Standard (2)	Estimated Works Cost (£ million) (3)	Approximate Length (Miles)
A380 Torbay - A38			
Trunking and Improvements	D2	26	8
A417/A419 Swindon - Gloucester			
Blunsdon Bypass	D2	5	1
Latton to Wilts/Gloucs Boundary*	D2	6	2
Stratton and Cirencester Bypass*	D2	16	7
Stratton to Crickley Hill	D2	13	9
West of M5 to Elmbridge Court	D2	2	2
A420 Oxford - Swindon			
Cumnor Hill to Kingston Bagpuize Improvement	D2	12	4
Southmoor to Shrivenham Bypass Improvement	D2	40	14
A428 Northampton - East of Bedford			
A1 to Great Barford Bypass Dualling	D2	3	2
A453 Nottingham - M1			
M1 to Clifton Improvement	D2	11	4
A465 Hereford - Welsh Border			
Llangua to Pontrilas Improvement	S	3	1
A500 Stoke on Trent - M6			
City Road and Stoke Road Junction Improvements, Stoke on Trent	D3/D2	16	1
A516 Derby - Uttoxeter			
North of Etwall Improvement	D2/S	2	1
A523 Ashbourne - Manchester			
Leek Bypass	S	8	5
Corridor Improvements Poynton-Macclesfield	S	5	3
A550 Merseyside - Welsh Border			
Ledsham to M53 Improvement	D2	3	2
A570 St. Helens - Southport			
Ormskirk Bypass	S	16	6
Scarisbrook and Pinfold Bypass	D2	10	3
A580 Liverpool - Manchester			
Corridor Improvements	D2	15	19
A590 Kendal - Barrow-in-Furness			
Ulverston to Dalton Bypass	D2	6	2
Corridor Improvements	S	1	1
A595/A596 Carlisle - Barrow-in-Furness			
Carlisle Southern Bypass	S	6	4
Parton to Lillyhall Improvement	S	9	3
A604 Cambridge - Huntingdon			
Huntingdon to Bar Hill Widening	D3	20	8
Huntingdon Link (A604 to A1)	D2	20	6

	Proposed Standard (2)	Estimated Works Cost (£ million) (3)	Approximate Length (Miles)
A650 Keighley - Bradford			
Hard Ings Road, Keighley	D2	5	1
A1033 East of Hull			
Hedon Road Improvement Stage 2	D2	9	2
A1079 York - Hull			
Shiptonthorpe Bypass	S	1	1
A1237 York Bypass			
York Northern Bypass (A19 - A64) Improvement	D2	8	8
A6120 Leeds Outer Ring Road			
Seacroft and Crossgates Bypass	D2	11	5

New routes/schemes

	Proposed Standard	Estimated Works Cost (£ million)	Approximate Length (Miles)
East West Route Aylesbury-A12	D2	123	46
comprising:			
A418 West of Aylesbury to East of Wing			
A5-A1 Link			
A1 to Stansted			
A120 Braintree to A12			
M1 to M62 Link (Wakefield - Kirklees)	D2	54	12
M56 to A6(M) Link (Manchester Airport)	D2	30	8
Exeter Northern Bypass	D2	53	7
Leicester Eastern Bypass (A6-A46)	D2/S	45	8
Poole Harbour - A31 Trunking and Improvements	D2/S	40	10

(1) The route titles shown (eg M1 London - Leeds) indicate broadly the extent of the route. The descriptions of the individual sections (eg widening between Junctions 6A - 32) show in general terms the location and nature of improvements proposed: they are not specifications of individual schemes. In cases where the dualling or improvement of a whole route is listed, this may incorporate existing schemes. Corridor Improvements refer to one or more small schemes to upgrade a route or part of it. Details of schemes already in the trunk road programme are listed in 'Policy for Roads in England: 1987' (Cm 125).

(2) Proposed standard is that indicated by traffic levels at current planning stage: this may change as the scheme progresses. The various standards are as follows:

   D4 dual carriageway, four lanes
   D3 dual carriageway, three lanes
   D2 dual carriageway, two lanes
   S   single carriageway

Widening schemes will usually include junction improvements, and may also involve the provision of separate lanes linking junctions (collector-distributor links). In some cases new off line routes may be an alternative to carriageway widening.

(3) November 1987 prices excluding VAT

* Extension of existing scheme

TABLE 2: PROPOSED STUDIES

Major Routes/Corridors

Location	Description
A1 Stamford to central A1(M) section south of Doncaster	Full review of strategic needs of corridor, including consideration of motorway status
Hook Moor to A1(M) section south of Darlington	Review of longer term needs, including consideration of motorway status
Northern A1(M) section (Darlington-Sunderland)	Study of future capacity of route
Trans-Pennine	Provision of additional capacity between south Lancashire and Yorkshire
Lower Thames Crossing	Relief to east side of M25, between Kent and Essex
East-West Kent - Hampshire	East-west strategic route, between Kent and Hampshire
M3 - M40 Link	Relieve pressure on SW quadrant of M25
A38 Exeter-Plymouth	Assessment of needs of whole route, including consideration of motorway status and new Tamar Crossing
A30/A303 M3 to Penzance	Assessment of needs of whole route, including links to Falmouth
A31/A35 Southampton-Exeter	Assessment of needs of whole route
M11	Review of existing motorway

Route Assessment and Scheme Identification Studies

M1 - A46 Link South of Nottingham

M25/M26 Interchange

M27/M271 Links and Junctions

A2   Bean to M2

A4/A36 South of Bath

A5   Old Stratford to M42

A10   Hoddesdon to Cambridge

A21   East Sussex

A38   Derby Ring Road Junctions

A45   Tollbar End Junction

A49   South of Ashton Bypass to Ross-onWye

A57   M1 to A1 (Worksop)

A64   Tadcaster to York

A428   Bedford to Northampton

ANNEX

1989 NATIONAL TRAFFIC FORECASTS

1. The new 1989 National Road Traffic Forecasts (NRTF)* supersede those published in 1984. Economic growth has been higher than was assumed for the 1984 forecasts. Largely as a result of this traffic has grown faster than was predicted. Traffic in 1988 was 27 per cent higher than in 1983 compared with a forecast growth of between 9 and 16 per cent.

2. The 1989 forecasts take a more optimistic view of future economic growth, reflecting the long-term structural improvements achieved in the economy. The forecasts assume that Gross Domestic Product will grow from its 1988 level by 26 to 46 per cent by the year 2000 and by between 101 and 215 per cent by 2025.

3. Income growth is the major determinant of the new forecasts; future fuel prices and demographic factors exert a small influence. Since future levels of income and fuel prices cannot be predicted with precision, the traffic growth forecasts are presented as a range, with the upper and lower bounds based on optimistic and pessimistic combinations of assumptions of growth in GDP and fuel prices. The high and low forecasts are equally possible outcomes.

4. The new forecasts for growth in traffic on all roads in Great Britain are set out in the following table.

FORECAST INCREASE IN VEHICLE MILES (%) 1988 - 2025

	Low	High
Cars	82	134
Light goods vehicles	101	215
Heavy goods vehicles	67	141
Buses and coaches	0	0
ALL TRAFFIC	**83**	**142**

In 1988 motor vehicle traffic was 205 billion vehicle miles, of which cars were 82.4 per cent, light goods vehicles 8.9 per cent, heavy goods vehicles 7.6 per cent and buses and coaches 1.1 per cent.

5. The above forecasts will be used in appraising motorway and trunk road schemes. They will play an important role in the assessment of whether the benefits from a scheme over its lifetime justify the initial cost and the standard of provision.

* National Road Traffic Forecasts (Great Britain) 1989, HMSO (to be published June 1989)

Bebington Reference Library